This wine journal was begun ....

Northwest Wine Journal

TERI CITTERMAN

SASQUATCH BOOKS
SEATTLE

This journal could not have been completed without the help of Andy Perdue, Ingo Grady, Bob Betz, Jim Bernau, and Allen Shoup.

Printed in Singapore by Star Standard Industries Pte Ltd.

Published by Sasquatch Books

Distributed by PGW/Perseus

15 14 13 12 11 10 09 08   9 8 7 6 5 4 3 2 1

Cover photograph: Brian Sprout (Osoyoos Larose Vineyard)

Cover design: Rosebud Eustace

Interior design and composition: Rosebud Eustace

ISBN-10: 1-57061-569-1

ISBN-13: 978-1-57061-569-6

Sasquatch Books

119 South Main Street, Suite 400

Seattle, WA 98104

(206) 467-4300

www.sasquatchbooks.com

custserv@sasquatchbooks.com

Previous page photo credit: *Osoyoos Larose Vineyard (Brian Sprout)*

Following page photo credit: *Naramata Vineyard (© Laughingmango/Dreamstime.com)*

CONTENTS

We could, in the United States, make as great a variety of wines as are made in Europe; not exactly of the same kinds, but doubtless as good.

—THOMAS JEFFERSON

Introduction

Wine means different things to different people. For some, it's an excuse to gather; for others, a ticket to unwind. Some drink for their health, while others drink to impress. Whether they become more impressive the more they drink remains to be seen; nonetheless, under whichever circumstances you find a glass in your hand, drink to determine what you like most. Taste, jot some notes, taste again, and nod approvingly—or perhaps disapprovingly—depending on the case.

"But I don't really know what I like," some say.

That's why we drink—well some of us, anyway. Tasting lots of wine will help you determine what you like. Taste, track, and taste again. Write a note here and there so you can remember which aspects of the wine were memorable. Was it the juicy, jammy flavors? The sturdy structure? The crisp acidity?

The study of wine can be a simple plunge or a subtle transformation. The bottom line is, wine is that universal language that crosses borders and boundaries—that expresses something to everyone—whether you drink it, observe it, cook with it, or are baffled by it. Besides the bible, wine is one of the oldest icons in history that still evokes emotion.

So write a few notes when the first splash touches your tongue. Because it's likely, on certain occasions and some holidays, you won't always have the best recollection of which wine was nutty, peachy, or toasty—let alone which wines you drank at all.

NORTHWEST WINE REGION

Imagine tasting the first vintages produced in Bordeaux or Burgundy thousands of years ago—the smell of the new stone chateaux, the color of the grapes in the vineyards, the taste of the wine upon first sip.

It is rare to witness the birth of a viticultural region. But here in the Northwest, that is exactly what is happening. The Northwest wine region, including Washington, Oregon, Idaho, and British Columbia, is among the youngest and fastest-growing regions in the world, with soils ripe with minerals and nutrients characteristic of other great wine-growing regions.

Centuries ago, a series of dam breaks around Glacial Lake Missoula led to one of the greatest floods ever recorded. That catastrophic event dramatically changed the lay and composition of Northwest land. The flood formed the Columbia Gorge as we know it today, and created soils ideal for growing a variety of grapes.

Wine Taster's Tip

➠ Looking for a hard-to-find wine? Visit the winery in question's Web site and sign up for its mailing list.

Today, the region has close to a thousand wineries. Those that are recommended in this journal produce the region's most consistent, top-quality wines as determined by the local, national, and world-wide recognition they've received. Unlike the behemoth Chateau Ste. Michelle, most of the region's wineries are "boutique" in that their case production is low. Many are open to the public, but some maintain a low, restricted profile with highly sought-after wines that are often sold out.

Although Idaho is not covered at length in this journal, it would be remiss to completely overlook it. When you look beyond the rolling hills of Red Mountain and Horse Heaven Hills in Washington, farther east toward the sun you'll see some of the highest vineyards in the Northwest. Idaho is a small but growing part of the Northwest's wine industry, with just over 20 wineries. Like the established wine producing states that border it, all arrows point to go for the "Gem State." Watch carefully, because in no time, Idaho's canvas will be speckled with new wineries and vineyards.

TASTING WINE

Wine can be intimidating. Why? Because there's a language of wine that's all its own, and some people find comfort in knowing just enough of that language to make others feel, let's say, deficient. Words like *acidity*, *cru*, *balance*, *terroir*, and *brix* may seem meaningless on their own, but thrown into the context of wine tasting, they may be the key to the next best bottle.

The key is to taste and taste often. If you pay attention and jot a note here and there, you can't help but learn about what you're tasting. And the Northwest, in particular, makes it easy for wine enthusiasts to take away as much or as little knowledge as desired. When you saunter into one of the plethora of tasting rooms in this region, the pourer behind the counter might very well be the maker of the wine. That's the beauty of a fledgling industry: wine here is very accessible, and most winemakers are happy to talk to you about their wines. Another unique facet of the Northwest wine region is that the wine community is extremely cooperative and supportive—of each other and of customers. The goal here is simply to make great wine for great people to enjoy.

Wine Taster's Tip

➤ Heading east on your wine-sampling tour? Try these recommended Idaho wineries:

- Pond d'Oreille Winery
- Sawtooth Winery
- Ste. Chapelle
- Bitner Vineyards
- Hells Canyon
- Koenig
- Snake River Winery
- Williamson Vineyard
- Coeur d'Alene Cellars
- Indian Creek

Drink often . . . and drink Northwest!

APPROACH

Tasting wine can be as simple or as complicated as you want it to be— from a methodical process to slapdash drinking. Either way you're going to learn something, and when you do, you should write it down. But *what* should you write down?

Wine has a lot of aspects to consider: aroma, flavor, color, clarity, sweetness, acidity, bitterness, and structure, to name a few. The more you taste, the more you sharpen your senses to the wines that really resonate for you. So run, don't walk, to the nearest tasting room, and engage these senses: sight, smell, and taste. Follow the common idiom "swirl, sip, spit," and you're off!

First, look at the wine. What is the characteristic of its color? If it's white, is it clear or cloudy? If it's red, is it a ruby shade or dark purple? Swirling the wine allows air to mix with it, freeing the aromas to "move about the cabin." And while you're swirling, check out the body of the wine. A wine's viscosity is indicated by "legs" that run down the sides of the glass when swirled. And as in life, the slower the legs move, the more mature the wine is.

After visually assessing the wine, it's time to shove your nose deep within the glass and inhale. Fireworks? Or a whole lot of nothing? Are you smelling honey, pepper, gasoline, shoe leather, or something else?

Then take a sip. In a tasting room, you may hear a distinctive sucking sound from some enthusiastic tasters. Why? Truth be told, it could be for a variety of reasons, but gurgling and slurping are quite appropriate, even encouraged, wine etiquette. Like swirling, mixing in a bit of air through your teeth with a sip of wine allows the aroma and flavors to unravel in the mouth. It's a practiced art, however, and after you get the hang of it, you may find yourself rolling in air when you taste your coffee, water, juice, or even the milk at the bottom of the cereal bowl!

When you sip, notice how the wine hits the front, back, and sides of your tongue. Is it sweet? Does it burn? Then hold it in the center and slosh it around like mouthwash, as do the experts. Now how does it feel on your tongue? And once you swallow, how long do the flavors linger?

Write down everything you've observed about the wine's appearance, smell, and taste. Yes, there's a lot to capture, and you may wonder how many times can you write that the wine tasted like blackberries or vanilla . . . or shoe leather. In truth, there are lots of ways to describe the essence of the wine and sensations you've just experienced, and the

> ## Wine Taster's Tip
>
> *Terroir* means dirt, and *brix* (not to be confused with bris) is the level by which the sugar in the grape is measured.

more tasting you do, the more specific terms you'll be able to apply. The following are some common terms and characteristics that may help you tell the story of the wine you've just tasted.

Appearance—Color & Clarity

Red wines fade with age from deep red and purple hues to tawny (brick-like) colors; whites darken into golden browns. Terms to describe color might include *straw, yellow,* and *golden* for whites and *rose, deep red, purple, brick,* and anything in between for reds. Clarity is another aspect to the wine's appearance. Is the wine clear, dull, or cloudy?

Structure

When you taste wine, note whether it's big and bold, full and rich, fat and flabby (not enough acid), or thin and watery. Is it sweet, crisp, buttery, or dry? Does it seem young and tight (lacking in flavor and aroma) or aged and smooth? Is there an excess of tannins (bitter) or is it soft and velvety?

Aroma & Flavor

Does the wine smell fruity like strawberry, blackberry, or plum, or do you taste vegetable notes like green pepper or asparagus? Do you sense spice or pepper, or more herb-based smells like fresh-cut grass?

Need help pinpointing an aroma or flavor? Please see the chart on the opposite page for words and terms to describe common varietals found in the Northwest.

USING THIS JOURNAL

The three regional sections of this journal contain pages to record your notes on wineries visited, reds and whites tasted, and other observations of your wine tasting and touring adventures.

Northwest Wine Descriptors

Chardonnay	Sauvignon Blanc	Gewürztraminer	Pinot Gris	Riesling
Green apple	Fresh-cut grass	Grapefruit	Apricot	Mineral
White peach	Mineral	Citrus	Pear	Citrus
Citrus	Bell pepper	Rose	Green apple	Floral
Pineapple	Cat urine	Litchi	Citrus	Lemon/Lime
Buttery	Citrus	Passionfruit	Sweet spices	Grapefruit
Vanilla	Grapefruit	Spice	Nectarine	Herbal
Toasted Oak	Melon	Floral	Nutty	Apple

Cabernet Sauvignon	Cabernet Franc	Syrah	Merlot	Pinot Noir
Blackberry	Black currant	Black pepper	Cherry	Strawberry
Black currant	Blackberry	Red currant	Blackberry	Cherry
Tobacco	Mulberry	Licorice	Raspberry	Tar
Coffee	Tobacco	Smokey	Earthy	Barnyard
Plum	Herbal	Leather	Spice	Cranberry
Raspberry	Vanilla	Blackberry	Black olive	Clove
Cassis	Capsicum	Cherry	Chocolate	Earthy

WASHINGTON

Main Varietals

Merlot · Syrah ·
Cabernet Sauvignon ·
Chardonnay · Riesling

Appellations

Yakima Valley · Walla Walla
Valley · Red Mountain ·
Columbia Valley · Puget Sound ·
Columbia Gorge · Horse Heaven
Hills · Wahluke Slope ·
Rattlesnake Hills

Touring Highlights

Chateau Ste. Michelle ·
Fidélitas · Matthews Cellars ·
Woodward Canyon · L'Ecole
N° 41 · Betz Family Winery ·
DeLille Cellars · Thurston
Wolfe · Barnard Griffin ·
Barrister Winery · Maryhill
Winery

Red Willow Vineyard (Mike Sauer)

WASHINGTON

More than 500 wineries adorn the hillsides, mountains, and valleys of Washington State. While the majority are concentrated in the state's wine country in Eastern Washington, a wine enthusiast on the quest for wine need look no further than the wine bars and retailers of Seattle, a corridor of wineries in Woodinville, a cluster of wineries on the Olympic Peninsula, or a handful of wineries on the San Juan Islands. Head east, west, north, or south and it won't be long before you stumble into one of the countless tasting rooms—simple or sophisticated—offering visitors a chance to sample the wares.

Taste what's in a bottle of Washington wine, and you'll find a union of old-world structure with new-world fruit intensity. How is Washington wine able to achieve such a unique feat?

The answer lies in the land. Washington's vineyards are spread out across nine designated grape growing areas called appellations, or American Viticultural Areas (AVAs). Located in the heart of Eastern Washington, the state's largest AVA is the Columbia Valley, which is drier and less humid than most wine-growing regions around the world. These conditions result in stronger flavors in the wines, such as a Riesling's penetration, the black currant taste of a Cabernet Sauvignon, or the plum and chocolate of a Merlot. In addition, the reds show a solid structural integrity and the whites have lower sugars and higher total acidity, which makes for crisp, balanced wines.

New World and Old World

The terms *new world* and *old world* define the style in which the wine was made. Typically, European wines are referred to as old world, where the emphasis is on the land imparting particular flavors and qualities. Wines classified as new world tend to have bolder, fruitier flavors and aromas, and are often a combination of mixed and matched grapes using one particular varietal, but selected from different vineyards.

The Columbia Valley AVA

The Columbia Valley includes more than 16,000 acres of vineyards. Half of the state's smaller AVAs are located within the borders of the Columbia Valley: Yakima Valley, Red Mountain, Horse Heaven Hills, Wahluke Slope, and Walla Walla Valley. Yakima is home to more than 50 wineries, and further east, Walla Walla has more than 110 wineries.

Today, Washington ranks as the second-largest wine producer in the U.S. Washington winemakers have matured over the past several decades, developing their own methodology and understanding of the grapes, the land, and the wines they produce. Now they're taking those findings and translating them into distinct wine cellar protocols, adding to the increased quality of Washington wine.

In fact, the world took notice of Washington wine in 2006 when Quilceda Creek's 2002 and 2003 Cabernet Sauvignons joined an elite group by obtaining perfect scores in noted wine critic Robert Parker's prestigious 100-point wine-rating system. For the wine industry in Washington and the Northwest as a whole, this was a significant coup that laid the foundation for other wineries to build on.

Meanwhile, a new generation of winemakers is emerging. The region's wine pioneers are now watching their sons and daughters come into their own with a new enthusiasm and a keener knowledge of winemaking they've learned from the land.

Long Shadows Vintners (photo courtesy of Long Shadows Vintners)

Washington Wineries to Visit

Name:..

Location:..

Recommended by:..

Why go:..

....

....

Name:..

Location:..

Recommended by:..

Why go:..

....

....

Name:..

Location:..

Recommended by:..

Why go:..

....

....

Name:..

Location:..

Recommended by:..

Why go:..

....

Name:...

Location:..

Recommended by:..

Why go:..

....

....

Name:...

Location:..

Recommended by:..

Why go:..

....

....

Name:...

Location:..

Recommended by:..

Why go:..

....

....

Name:...

Location:..

Recommended by:..

Why go:..

....

Name:...

Location:...

Recommended by:...

Why go:..

....

....

Name:...

Location:...

Recommended by:...

Why go:..

....

....

Name:...

Location:...

Recommended by:...

Why go:..

....

....

Name:...

Location:...

Recommended by:...

Why go:..

....

Name:..

Location:..

Recommended by:..

Why go:...

....

....

Name:..

Location:..

Recommended by:..

Why go:...

....

....

Name:..

Location:..

Recommended by:..

Why go:...

....

....

Name:..

Location:..

Recommended by:..

Why go:...

....

Name:..

Location:..

Recommended by:..

Why go:..

....

....

Name:..

Location:..

Recommended by:..

Why go:..

....

....

Name:..

Location:..

Recommended by:..

Why go:..

....

....

Name:..

Location:..

Recommended by:..

Why go:..

....

Name:..

Location:...

Recommended by:...

Why go:...

....

....

Name:..

Location:...

Recommended by:...

Why go:...

....

....

Name:..

Location:...

Recommended by:...

Why go:...

....

....

Name:..

Location:...

Recommended by:...

Why go:...

....

Washington Reds

Winery:...

Region:...

Name of wine:...

Vintage:...

Price:...

Purchase date:..

Circle:

Cabernet Sauvignon	Cabernet Franc	Gamay Grenache
Merlot	Nebbiolo	Pinot Noir
Syrah	Sangiovese	Tempranillo
Zinfandel	Other........................	

Color:...

Structure:..

Aroma:...

Taste:...

Food pairings:...

....

....

Additional notes:...

....

....

Overall rating:

Drinkable   Recommended   Fantastic

Washington Reds

Winery:...

Region:...

Name of wine:...

Vintage:...

Price:...

Purchase date:...

Circle:

Cabernet Sauvignon	Cabernet Franc	Gamay Grenache
Merlot	Nebbiolo	Pinot Noir
Syrah	Sangiovese	Tempranillo
Zinfandel	Other........................	

Color:..

Structure:...

Aroma:..

Taste:..

Food pairings:...

....

....

Additional notes:...

....

....

Overall rating:

Drinkable   Recommended   Fantastic

Washington Reds

Winery:..

Region:..

Name of wine:..

Vintage:..

Price:..

Purchase date:..

Circle:

Cabernet Sauvignon	Cabernet Franc	Gamay Grenache
Merlot	Nebbiolo	Pinot Noir
Syrah	Sangiovese	Tempranillo
Zinfandel	Other........................	

Color:..

Structure:..

Aroma:..

Taste:..

Food pairings:..

....

....

Additional notes:..

....

....

Overall rating:

Drinkable   Recommended   Fantastic

Washington Reds

Winery:..

Region:..

Name of wine:..

Vintage:..

Price:..

Purchase date:..

Circle:

Cabernet Sauvignon	Cabernet Franc	Gamay Grenache
Merlot	Nebbiolo	Pinot Noir
Syrah	Sangiovese	Tempranillo
Zinfandel	Other.........................	

Color:..

Structure:..

Aroma:..

Taste:..

Food pairings:..

....

....

Additional notes:..

....

....

Overall rating:

Drinkable   Recommended   Fantastic

Washington Reds

Winery:..

Region:..

Name of wine:..

Vintage:..

Price:..

Purchase date:..

Circle:

Cabernet Sauvignon	Cabernet Franc	Gamay Grenache
Merlot	Nebbiolo	Pinot Noir
Syrah	Sangiovese	Tempranillo
Zinfandel	Other........................	

Color:..

Structure:..

Aroma:..

Taste:..

Food pairings:..

....

....

Additional notes:..

....

....

Overall rating:

Drinkable   Recommended   Fantastic

Washington Reds

Winery:..

Region:..

Name of wine:..

Vintage:..

Price:..

Purchase date:..

Circle:

Cabernet Sauvignon	Cabernet Franc	Gamay Grenache
Merlot	Nebbiolo	Pinot Noir
Syrah	Sangiovese	Tempranillo
Zinfandel	Other......................	

Color:..

Structure:..

Aroma:..

Taste:..

Food pairings:..

....

....

Additional notes:..

....

....

Overall rating:

Drinkable   Recommended   Fantastic

Washington Reds

Winery:...

Region:...

Name of wine:...

Vintage:..

Price:..

Purchase date:..

Circle:

Cabernet Sauvignon	Cabernet Franc	Gamay Grenache
Merlot	Nebbiolo	Pinot Noir
Syrah	Sangiovese	Tempranillo
Zinfandel	Other.........................	

Color:...

Structure:...

Aroma:...

Taste:...

Food pairings:..

....

....

Additional notes:...

....

....

Overall rating:

Drinkable   Recommended   Fantastic

Washington Reds

Winery:...

Region:...

Name of wine:...

Vintage:...

Price:...

Purchase date:...

Circle:

Cabernet Sauvignon	Cabernet Franc	Gamay Grenache
Merlot	Nebbiolo	Pinot Noir
Syrah	Sangiovese	Tempranillo
Zinfandel	Other.........................	

Color:...

Structure:...

Aroma:...

Taste:...

Food pairings:...

....

....

Additional notes:...

....

....

Overall rating:

Drinkable   Recommended   Fantastic

Washington Reds

Winery:..

Region:..

Name of wine:..

Vintage:..

Price:..

Purchase date:..

Circle:

Cabernet Sauvignon	Cabernet Franc	Gamay Grenache
Merlot	Nebbiolo	Pinot Noir
Syrah	Sangiovese	Tempranillo
Zinfandel	Other........................	

Color:..

Structure:..

Aroma:..

Taste:..

Food pairings:..

....

....

Additional notes:..

....

....

Overall rating:

Drinkable   Recommended   Fantastic

Washington Reds

Winery:...

Region:...

Name of wine:...

Vintage:...

Price:...

Purchase date:..

Circle:

Cabernet Sauvignon	Cabernet Franc	Gamay Grenache
Merlot	Nebbiolo	Pinot Noir
Syrah	Sangiovese	Tempranillo
Zinfandel	Other..........................	

Color:..

Structure:..

Aroma:...

Taste:...

Food pairings:...

....

....

Additional notes:..

....

....

Overall rating:

Drinkable   Recommended   Fantastic

Washington Reds

Winery:...

Region:...

Name of wine:...

Vintage:...

Price:...

Purchase date:...

Circle:

Cabernet Sauvignon	Cabernet Franc	Gamay Grenache
Merlot	Nebbiolo	Pinot Noir
Syrah	Sangiovese	Tempranillo
Zinfandel	Other.........................	

Color:..

Structure:...

Aroma:...

Taste:..

Food pairings:...

....

....

Additional notes:...

....

....

Overall rating:

Drinkable   Recommended   Fantastic

Washington Reds

Winery:...

Region:...

Name of wine:...

Vintage:...

Price:...

Purchase date:...

Circle:

Cabernet Sauvignon	Cabernet Franc	Gamay Grenache
Merlot	Nebbiolo	Pinot Noir
Syrah	Sangiovese	Tempranillo
Zinfandel	Other........................	

Color:...

Structure:...

Aroma:...

Taste:...

Food pairings:...

....

....

Additional notes:...

....

....

Overall rating:

Drinkable   Recommended   Fantastic

Washington Reds

Winery:...

Region:...

Name of wine:...

Vintage:..

Price:..

Purchase date:..

Circle:

Cabernet Sauvignon	Cabernet Franc	Gamay Grenache
Merlot	Nebbiolo	Pinot Noir
Syrah	Sangiovese	Tempranillo
Zinfandel	Other.........................	

Color:...

Structure:..

Aroma:..

Taste:..

Food pairings:...

....

....

Additional notes:...

....

....

Overall rating:

Drinkable   Recommended   Fantastic

Washington Reds

Winery:...

Region:...

Name of wine:..

Vintage:...

Price:...

Purchase date:..

Circle:

Cabernet Sauvignon	Cabernet Franc	Gamay Grenache
Merlot	Nebbiolo	Pinot Noir
Syrah	Sangiovese	Tempranillo
Zinfandel	Other.........................	

Color:..

Structure:..

Aroma:..

Taste:..

Food pairings:..

....

....

Additional notes:..

....

....

Overall rating:

Drinkable　　　　　　Recommended　　　　　　Fantastic

Hedges Family Estate (photo courtesy of Hedges Family Estate)

Red Willow Vineyard (Mike Sauer)

Washington Whites

Winery:...

Region:...

Name of wine:..

Vintage:..

Price:..

Purchase date:..

Circle:

Chardonnay	Chenin Blanc	Gewürztraminer	Muscat
Pinot Gris	Riesling	Sauvignon Blanc	Sémillon
Viognier	Other........................		

Color:...

Structure:...

Clarity:...

Aroma:...

Taste:...

Food pairings:..

....

....

Additional notes:...

....

....

Overall rating:

Drinkable   Recommended   Fantastic

Washington Whites

Winery:..

Region:..

Name of wine:..

Vintage:..

Price:..

Purchase date:...

Circle:

Chardonnay	Chenin Blanc	Gewürztraminer	Muscat
Pinot Gris	Riesling	Sauvignon Blanc	Sémillon
Viognier	Other........................		

Color:...

Structure:..

Clarity:...

Aroma:...

Taste:...

Food pairings:..

....

....

Additional notes:...

....

....

Overall rating:

Drinkable   Recommended   Fantastic

Washington Whites

Winery:..

Region:...

Name of wine:...

Vintage:...

Price:...

Purchase date:...

Circle:

Chardonnay	Chenin Blanc	Gewürztraminer	Muscat
Pinot Gris	Riesling	Sauvignon Blanc	Sémillon
Viognier	Other........................		

Color:..

Structure:..

Clarity:..

Aroma:..

Taste:..

Food pairings:...

....

....

Additional notes:...

....

....

Overall rating:
Drinkable   Recommended   Fantastic

Washington Whites

Winery:...

Region:...

Name of wine:..

Vintage:..

Price:..

Purchase date:..

Circle:

Chardonnay	Chenin Blanc	Gewürztraminer	Muscat
Pinot Gris	Riesling	Sauvignon Blanc	Sémillon
Viognier	Other........................		

Color:...

Structure:...

Clarity:...

Aroma:...

Taste:...

Food pairings:..

....

....

Additional notes:...

....

....

Overall rating:

Drinkable   Recommended   Fantastic

Washington Whites

Winery:..

Region:..

Name of wine:..

Vintage:..

Price:..

Purchase date:..

Circle:

Chardonnay	Chenin Blanc	Gewürztraminer	Muscat
Pinot Gris	Riesling	Sauvignon Blanc	Sémillon
Viognier	Other........................		

Color:..

Structure:..

Clarity:..

Aroma:..

Taste:..

Food pairings:..

....

....

Additional notes:..

....

....

Overall rating:

Drinkable   Recommended   Fantastic

Washington Whites

Winery:...

Region:...

Name of wine:...

Vintage:...

Price:...

Purchase date:..

Circle:

Chardonnay	Chenin Blanc	Gewürztraminer	Muscat
Pinot Gris	Riesling	Sauvignon Blanc	Sémillon
Viognier	Other..................		

Color:..

Structure:..

Clarity:..

Aroma:...

Taste:...

Food pairings:..

....

....

Additional notes:...

....

....

Overall rating:
Drinkable   Recommended   Fantastic

Washington Whites

Winery:...

Region:...

Name of wine:...

Vintage:...

Price:...

Purchase date:..

Circle:

Chardonnay	Chenin Blanc	Gewürztraminer	Muscat
Pinot Gris	Riesling	Sauvignon Blanc	Sémillon
Viognier	Other........................		

Color:..

Structure:...

Clarity:..

Aroma:..

Taste:..

Food pairings:..

....

....

Additional notes:...

....

....

Overall rating:

Drinkable   Recommended   Fantastic

Washington Whites

Winery:...

Region:...

Name of wine:...

Vintage:..

Price:..

Purchase date:...

Circle:

Chardonnay	Chenin Blanc	Gewürztraminer	Muscat
Pinot Gris	Riesling	Sauvignon Blanc	Sémillon
Viognier	Other........................		

Color:...

Structure:...

Clarity:...

Aroma:...

Taste:...

Food pairings:..

....

....

Additional notes:...

....

....

Overall rating:

Drinkable   Recommended   Fantastic

Washington Whites

Winery:..

Region:..

Name of wine:..

Vintage:..

Price:..

Purchase date:...

Circle:

Chardonnay	Chenin Blanc	Gewürztraminer	Muscat
Pinot Gris	Riesling	Sauvignon Blanc	Sémillon
Viognier	Other.........................		

Color:...

Structure:...

Clarity:...

Aroma:...

Taste:...

Food pairings:...

....

....

Additional notes:..

....

....

Overall rating:

Drinkable   Recommended   Fantastic

Washington Whites

Winery:..

Region:..

Name of wine:..

Vintage:...

Price:...

Purchase date:...

Circle:

Chardonnay   Chenin Blanc   Gewürztraminer   Muscat
Pinot Gris   Riesling   Sauvignon Blanc   Sémillon
Viognier   Other.........................

Color:..

Structure:..

Clarity:...

Aroma:...

Taste:..

Food pairings:..

....

....

Additional notes:..

....

....

Overall rating:
Drinkable   Recommended   Fantastic

Washington Whites

Winery:..

Region:..

Name of wine:...

Vintage:..

Price:...

Purchase date:...

Circle:

Chardonnay	Chenin Blanc	Gewürztraminer	Muscat
Pinot Gris	Riesling	Sauvignon Blanc	Sémillon
Viognier	Other.........................		

Color:..

Structure:...

Clarity:..

Aroma:..

Taste:..

Food pairings:...

....

....

Additional notes:...

....

....

Overall rating:

Drinkable   Recommended   Fantastic

Washington Whites

Winery:...

Region:...

Name of wine:...

Vintage:...

Price:...

Purchase date:..

Circle:

Chardonnay	Chenin Blanc	Gewürztraminer	Muscat
Pinot Gris	Riesling	Sauvignon Blanc	Sémillon
Viognier	Other.........................		

Color:..

Structure:..

Clarity:..

Aroma:...

Taste:...

Food pairings:..

....

....

Additional notes:...

....

....

Overall rating:

Drinkable   Recommended   Fantastic

Washington Whites

Winery:..

Region:..

Name of wine:...

Vintage:...

Price:..

Purchase date:..

Circle:

Chardonnay	Chenin Blanc	Gewürztraminer	Muscat
Pinot Gris	Riesling	Sauvignon Blanc	Sémillon
Viognier	Other.........................		

Color:..

Structure:...

Clarity:...

Aroma:..

Taste:..

Food pairings:..

....

....

Additional notes:..

....

....

Overall rating:

Drinkable   Recommended   Fantastic

Washington Whites

Winery:..

Region:..

Name of wine:..

Vintage:..

Price:..

Purchase date:..

Circle:

Chardonnay	Chenin Blanc	Gewürztraminer	Muscat
Pinot Gris	Riesling	Sauvignon Blanc	Sémillon
Viognier	Other...........................		

Color:...

Structure:...

Clarity:...

Aroma:...

Taste:...

Food pairings:...

....

....

Additional notes:..

....

....

Overall rating:

Drinkable   Recommended   Fantastic

Red Willow Vineyard (Mike Sauer)

Hedges Family Estate (photo courtesy of Hedges Family Estate)

Notes

OREGON

Main Varietals

Pinot Noir · Pinot Gris ·
Chardonnay · Merlot

Appellations

Willamette Valley · Chehalem
Mountains · Yamhill-Carlton
District · Ribbon Ridge ·
Dundee Hills · McMinnville ·
Eola-Amity Hills · Umpqua
Valley · Red Hills Douglas
County · Rogue Valley ·
Applegate Valley · Southern
Oregon · Columbia Gorge ·
Columbia Valley · Walla Walla
Valley · Snake River Valley

Touring Highlights

Penner-Ash Cellars · Patricia
Green Cellars · Archery
Summit · Abacela Winery ·
Bethel Heights · Sineann ·
Troon Vineyard · Privé
Vineyard · Willamette Valley
Vineyards · Adelsheim Cellars

*Vineyard and tasting room in the Willamette
Valley (© iStockphoto.com/Tatiana Boyle)*

OREGON

Visiting Oregon's wineries offers a relaxed, personal experience. The volume of tourists that comes through the tasting rooms is much smaller than that of large wineries in other states, and wine enthusiasts experience Oregon wine face-to-face with local winemakers.

In Oregon, winemakers to the south—California—and to the east—France—influenced the success of the state's wine industry. The first rootstalks planted in Oregon came from California and France, with Chardonnay being the predominant grape. With help from Californian and French winemakers—and benefiting from Oregon's cooler climate—early Oregon Chardonnays showed similar characteristics to whites from Burgundy.

Building on the success of their Chardonnays, Oregon winemakers first commercially grew Pinot Noir in the early 1960s, adding clones from California and France by the mid-'90s. Combining true winemaking collaboration with lots of sweat and patience, Oregon blossomed into what is now a world-renowned Pinot Noir–producing region.

The Willamette Valley AVA

Most Oregon wines come from the prolific Willamette Valley. Just south of Portland, the Willamette Valley AVA is 150 miles long and 60 miles wide, with the state's largest concentration of wineries—more than 200 amidst 10,000 acres of vineyards. It is the most expansive AVA in Oregon and encompasses six sub-appellations: Dundee Hills, Eola-Amity Hills, McMinnville, Ribbon Ridge, Yamhill-Carlton District, and Chehalem Mountains.

And then there was Hollywood.

The movie *Sideways*—where the main character, wine connoisseur Miles, describes his beloved but delicate Pinot as "thin-skinned, temperamental, ripens early . . . not a survivor like Cabernet"—has had a long-lasting impact on Oregon's burgeoning industry. What could have been just 15 seconds of fame turned into a ticket to the worldwide wine stage. The movie boosted popular awareness of Pinot Noir as a varietal, so its popularity skyrocketed, which lead to an increased awareness of Oregon as a wine-growing region and greater demand for Oregon Pinot Noirs. Since then, Oregon has basked in this spotlight while improving its consistency in producing high-quality wines.

Oregon's wine industry tends to be collaborative, in the sense that ideas are shared openly. Historically, people in the industry have worked together to improve the quality of wines and promote the region as a whole. To outsiders, the state of Oregon has a reputation for being environmentally conscious and is known for alternative thinking. This carries over to its wine industry, which supports environmental initiatives and is a leader in environmental programs and energy conservation. Like wineries in neighboring states, many Oregon vineyards practice sustainable and organic farming, and Oregon leads the Northwest in certified biodynamic farming, a method of organic farming that treats farms as unified and individual organisms.

If you ask anyone who drinks or produces Oregon wine, the outlook for the region is bright: more and more small winemakers will continue to produce exceptional wine—just as is done in the hills of Burgundy in France.

Abacela (Paula C. Caudill)

Willamette Valley Vineyards (Jon Mason Photography)

Oregon Wineries to Visit

Name:..

Location:..

Recommended by:..

Why go:...

....

....

Name:..

Location:..

Recommended by:..

Why go:...

....

....

Name:..

Location:..

Recommended by:..

Why go:...

....

....

Name:..

Location:..

Recommended by:..

Why go:...

....

Name:..

Location:..

Recommended by:...

Why go:...

....

....

Name:..

Location:..

Recommended by:...

Why go:...

....

....

Name:..

Location:..

Recommended by:...

Why go:...

....

....

Name:..

Location:..

Recommended by:...

Why go:...

....

Name:..

Location:..

Recommended by:...

Why go:..

....

....

Name:..

Location:..

Recommended by:...

Why go:..

....

....

Name:..

Location:..

Recommended by:...

Why go:..

....

....

Name:..

Location:..

Recommended by:...

Why go:..

....

Name:...

Location:...

Recommended by:...

Why go:...

....

....

Name:...

Location:...

Recommended by:...

Why go:...

....

....

Name:...

Location:...

Recommended by:...

Why go:...

....

....

Name:...

Location:...

Recommended by:...

Why go:...

....

Name:...

Location:..

Recommended by:...

Why go:...

....

....

Name:...

Location:..

Recommended by:...

Why go:...

....

....

Name:...

Location:..

Recommended by:...

Why go:...

....

....

Name:...

Location:..

Recommended by:...

Why go:...

....

Name:...

Location:...

Recommended by:..

Why go:..

....

....

Name:...

Location:...

Recommended by:..

Why go:..

....

....

Name:...

Location:...

Recommended by:..

Why go:..

....

....

Name:...

Location:...

Recommended by:..

Why go:..

....

Oregon Reds

Winery:...

Region:...

Name of wine:...

Vintage:..

Price:..

Purchase date:...

Circle:

Cabernet Sauvignon	Cabernet Franc	Gamay Grenache
Merlot	Nebbiolo	Pinot Noir
Syrah	Sangiovese	Tempranillo
Zinfandel	Other........................	

Color:...

Structure:...

Aroma:...

Taste:...

Food pairings:...

....

....

Additional notes:...

....

....

Overall rating:

Drinkable   Recommended   Fantastic

Oregon Reds

Winery:...

Region:...

Name of wine:...

Vintage:...

Price:...

Purchase date:...

Circle:

Cabernet Sauvignon	Cabernet Franc	Gamay Grenache
Merlot	Nebbiolo	Pinot Noir
Syrah	Sangiovese	Tempranillo
Zinfandel	Other...........................	

Color:..

Structure:...

Aroma:...

Taste:...

Food pairings:..

....

....

Additional notes:...

....

....

Overall rating:

Drinkable　　　　　Recommended　　　　　Fantastic

Oregon Reds

Winery:...

Region:...

Name of wine:...

Vintage:...

Price:...

Purchase date:..

Circle:

Cabernet Sauvignon   Cabernet Franc   Gamay Grenache
Merlot   Nebbiolo   Pinot Noir
Syrah   Sangiovese   Tempranillo
Zinfandel   Other............................

Color:..

Structure:...

Aroma:..

Taste:..

Food pairings:..

....

....

Additional notes:...

....

....

Overall rating:
Drinkable   Recommended   Fantastic

Oregon Reds

Winery:..

Region:..

Name of wine:..

Vintage:..

Price:..

Purchase date:...

Circle:

Cabernet Sauvignon	Cabernet Franc	Gamay Grenache
Merlot	Nebbiolo	Pinot Noir
Syrah	Sangiovese	Tempranillo
Zinfandel	Other...........................	

Color:...

Structure:..

Aroma:..

Taste:..

Food pairings:..

....

....

Additional notes:...

....

....

Overall rating:

Drinkable   Recommended   Fantastic

Oregon Reds

Winery:...

Region:...

Name of wine:..

Vintage:..

Price:..

Purchase date:...

Circle:

Cabernet Sauvignon	Cabernet Franc	Gamay Grenache
Merlot	Nebbiolo	Pinot Noir
Syrah	Sangiovese	Tempranillo
Zinfandel	Other........................	

Color:...

Structure:...

Aroma:...

Taste:...

Food pairings:..

....

....

Additional notes:...

....

....

Overall rating:

Drinkable   Recommended   Fantastic

Oregon Reds

Winery:...

Region:...

Name of wine:...

Vintage:...

Price:...

Purchase date:..

Circle:

Cabernet Sauvignon   Cabernet Franc   Gamay Grenache

Merlot   Nebbiolo   Pinot Noir

Syrah   Sangiovese   Tempranillo

Zinfandel   Other.........................

Color:..

Structure:..

Aroma:...

Taste:...

Food pairings:...

....

....

Additional notes:..

....

....

Overall rating:

Drinkable   Recommended   Fantastic

Oregon Reds

Winery:...

Region:...

Name of wine:..

Vintage:...

Price:...

Purchase date:...

Circle:

Cabernet Sauvignon	Cabernet Franc	Gamay Grenache
Merlot	Nebbiolo	Pinot Noir
Syrah	Sangiovese	Tempranillo
Zinfandel	Other.........................	

Color:..

Structure:..

Aroma:...

Taste:...

Food pairings:..

....

....

Additional notes:...

....

....

Overall rating:

Drinkable   Recommended   Fantastic

Oregon Reds

Winery:...

Region:...

Name of wine:..

Vintage:...

Price:...

Purchase date:...

Circle:

Cabernet Sauvignon	Cabernet Franc	Gamay Grenache
Merlot	Nebbiolo	Pinot Noir
Syrah	Sangiovese	Tempranillo
Zinfandel	Other...........................	

Color:..

Structure:..

Aroma:...

Taste:...

Food pairings:...

....

....

Additional notes:...

....

....

Overall rating:

Drinkable   Recommended   Fantastic

Oregon Reds

Winery:...

Region:...

Name of wine:..

Vintage:..

Price:...

Purchase date:...

Circle:

Cabernet Sauvignon	Cabernet Franc	Gamay Grenache
Merlot	Nebbiolo	Pinot Noir
Syrah	Sangiovese	Tempranillo
Zinfandel	Other..........................	

Color:...

Structure:...

Aroma:...

Taste:...

Food pairings:...

....

....

Additional notes:..

....

....

Overall rating:

Drinkable   Recommended   Fantastic

Oregon Reds

Winery:...

Region:...

Name of wine:...

Vintage:...

Price:...

Purchase date:...

Circle:

Cabernet Sauvignon	Cabernet Franc	Gamay Grenache
Merlot	Nebbiolo	Pinot Noir
Syrah	Sangiovese	Tempranillo
Zinfandel	Other............................	

Color:...

Structure:..

Aroma:...

Taste:...

Food pairings:...

....

....

Additional notes:..

....

....

Overall rating:
Drinkable   Recommended   Fantastic

67

Oregon Reds

Winery:..

Region:..

Name of wine:...

Vintage:..

Price:..

Purchase date:...

Circle:

Cabernet Sauvignon	Cabernet Franc	Gamay Grenache
Merlot	Nebbiolo	Pinot Noir
Syrah	Sangiovese	Tempranillo
Zinfandel	Other..........................	

Color:...

Structure:...

Aroma:..

Taste:..

Food pairings:..

....

....

Additional notes:..

....

....

Overall rating:

Drinkable   Recommended   Fantastic

Oregon Reds

Winery:...

Region:...

Name of wine:..

Vintage:..

Price:..

Purchase date:...

Circle:

Cabernet Sauvignon	Cabernet Franc	Gamay Grenache
Merlot	Nebbiolo	Pinot Noir
Syrah	Sangiovese	Tempranillo
Zinfandel	Other..........................	

Color:...

Structure:...

Aroma:...

Taste:...

Food pairings:...

....

....

Additional notes:...

....

....

Overall rating:

Drinkable   Recommended   Fantastic

Oregon Reds

Winery:..

Region:..

Name of wine:..

Vintage:..

Price:..

Purchase date:..

Circle:

Cabernet Sauvignon	Cabernet Franc	Gamay Grenache
Merlot	Nebbiolo	Pinot Noir
Syrah	Sangiovese	Tempranillo
Zinfandel	Other........................	

Color:..

Structure:..

Aroma:..

Taste:..

Food pairings:..

....

....

Additional notes:..

....

....

Overall rating:

Drinkable   Recommended   Fantastic

Oregon Reds

Winery:...

Region:..

Name of wine:..

Vintage:..

Price:..

Purchase date:...

Circle:

Cabernet Sauvignon	Cabernet Franc	Gamay Grenache
Merlot	Nebbiolo	Pinot Noir
Syrah	Sangiovese	Tempranillo
Zinfandel	Other.........................	

Color:...

Structure:...

Aroma:..

Taste:..

Food pairings:..

....

....

Additional notes:...

....

....

Overall rating:

Drinkable   Recommended   Fantastic

Oregon vineyard in early morning fog (© Jeannehatch/Dreamstime.com)

Wine bottles on display (© Stockbyte/PunchStock.com)

Oregon Whites

Winery:..

Region:..

Name of wine:..

Vintage:..

Price:..

Purchase date:...

Circle:

Chardonnay	Chenin Blanc	Gewürztraminer	Muscat
Pinot Gris	Riesling	Sauvignon Blanc	Sémillon
Viognier	Other........................		

Color:..

Structure:...

Clarity:..

Aroma:...

Taste:..

Food pairings:..

....

....

Additional notes:..

....

....

Overall rating:

Drinkable   Recommended   Fantastic

Oregon Whites

Winery:..

Region:..

Name of wine:..

Vintage:..

Price:..

Purchase date:...

Circle:

Chardonnay	Chenin Blanc	Gewürztraminer	Muscat
Pinot Gris	Riesling	Sauvignon Blanc	Sémillon
Viognier	Other........................		

Color:..

Structure:..

Clarity:..

Aroma:..

Taste:..

Food pairings:..

....

....

Additional notes:..

....

....

Overall rating:

Drinkable   Recommended   Fantastic

Oregon Whites

Winery:...

Region:...

Name of wine:...

Vintage:..

Price:..

Purchase date:...

Circle:

Chardonnay	Chenin Blanc	Gewürztraminer	Muscat
Pinot Gris	Riesling	Sauvignon Blanc	Sémillon
Viognier	Other........................		

Color:..

Structure:..

Clarity:..

Aroma:..

Taste:...

Food pairings:...

....

....

Additional notes:..

....

....

Overall rating:

Drinkable   Recommended   Fantastic

Oregon Whites

Winery:..

Region:..

Name of wine:..

Vintage:..

Price:..

Purchase date:..

Circle:

Chardonnay   Chenin Blanc   Gewürztraminer   Muscat
Pinot Gris   Riesling   Sauvignon Blanc   Sémillon
Viognier   Other..........................

Color:..

Structure:..

Clarity:..

Aroma:..

Taste:..

Food pairings:..

....

....

Additional notes:..

....

....

Overall rating:

Drinkable   Recommended   Fantastic

Oregon Whites

Winery:..

Region:..

Name of wine:...

Vintage:..

Price:...

Purchase date:..

Circle:

Chardonnay	Chenin Blanc	Gewürztraminer	Muscat
Pinot Gris	Riesling	Sauvignon Blanc	Sémillon
Viognier	Other..........................		

Color:...

Structure:..

Clarity:...

Aroma:..

Taste:..

Food pairings:...

....

....

Additional notes:..

....

....

Overall rating:

Drinkable   Recommended   Fantastic

Oregon Whites

Winery:..

Region:..

Name of wine:..

Vintage:..

Price:..

Purchase date:...

Circle:

Chardonnay	Chenin Blanc	Gewürztraminer	Muscat
Pinot Gris	Riesling	Sauvignon Blanc	Sémillon
Viognier	Other........................		

Color:..

Structure:..

Clarity:..

Aroma:..

Taste:..

Food pairings:...

....

....

Additional notes:...

....

....

Overall rating:

Drinkable   Recommended   Fantastic

Oregon Whites

Winery:...

Region:...

Name of wine:...

Vintage:..

Price:...

Purchase date:..

Circle:

Chardonnay	Chenin Blanc	Gewürztraminer	Muscat
Pinot Gris	Riesling	Sauvignon Blanc	Sémillon
Viognier	Other......................		

Color:...

Structure:...

Clarity:..

Aroma:...

Taste:...

Food pairings:...

....

....

Additional notes:...

....

....

Overall rating:

Drinkable   Recommended   Fantastic

Oregon Whites

Winery: ....

Region: ....

Name of wine: ....

Vintage: ....

Price: ....

Purchase date: ....

Circle:

Chardonnay	Chenin Blanc	Gewürztraminer	Muscat
Pinot Gris	Riesling	Sauvignon Blanc	Sémillon
Viognier	Other........................		

Color: ....

Structure: ....

Clarity: ....

Aroma: ....

Taste: ....

Food pairings: ....

....

....

Additional notes: ....

....

....

Overall rating:

Drinkable   Recommended   Fantastic

Oregon Whites

Winery:..

Region:..

Name of wine:...

Vintage:..

Price:..

Purchase date:..

Circle:

Chardonnay	Chenin Blanc	Gewürztraminer	Muscat
Pinot Gris	Riesling	Sauvignon Blanc	Sémillon
Viognier	Other........................		

Color:...

Structure:...

Clarity:...

Aroma:..

Taste:...

Food pairings:..

....

....

Additional notes:...

....

....

Overall rating:

Drinkable   Recommended   Fantastic

Oregon Whites

Winery:...

Region:...

Name of wine:...

Vintage:...

Price:...

Purchase date:..

Circle:

Chardonnay	Chenin Blanc	Gewürztraminer	Muscat
Pinot Gris	Riesling	Sauvignon Blanc	Sémillon
Viognier	Other..........................		

Color:...

Structure:...

Clarity:..

Aroma:...

Taste:...

Food pairings:...

....

....

Additional notes:..

....

....

Overall rating:

Drinkable   Recommended   Fantastic

Oregon Whites

Winery:...

Region:...

Name of wine:...

Vintage:...

Price:...

Purchase date:...

Circle:

Chardonnay	Chenin Blanc	Gewürztraminer	Muscat
Pinot Gris	Riesling	Sauvignon Blanc	Sémillon
Viognier	Other........................		

Color:..

Structure:..

Clarity:..

Aroma:..

Taste:..

Food pairings:...

....

....

Additional notes:..

....

....

Overall rating:

Drinkable   Recommended   Fantastic

Oregon Whites

Winery:..

Region:..

Name of wine:...

Vintage:...

Price:..

Purchase date:...

Circle:

Chardonnay   Chenin Blanc   Gewürztraminer   Muscat
Pinot Gris   Riesling   Sauvignon Blanc   Sémillon
Viognier   Other...........................

Color:...

Structure:..

Clarity:...

Aroma:..

Taste:..

Food pairings:...

....

....

Additional notes:..

....

....

Overall rating:

Drinkable   Recommended   Fantastic

Oregon Whites

Winery:..

Region:..

Name of wine:..

Vintage:...

Price:...

Purchase date:...

Circle:

Chardonnay	Chenin Blanc	Gewürztraminer	Muscat
Pinot Gris	Riesling	Sauvignon Blanc	Sémillon
Viognier	Other..........................		

Color:..

Structure:..

Clarity:..

Aroma:..

Taste:..

Food pairings:...

....

....

Additional notes:...

....

....

Overall rating:

Drinkable   Recommended   Fantastic

Oregon Whites

Winery:..

Region:..

Name of wine:..

Vintage:..

Price:..

Purchase date:..

Circle:

Chardonnay	Chenin Blanc	Gewürztraminer	Muscat
Pinot Gris	Riesling	Sauvignon Blanc	Sémillon
Viognier	Other...........................		

Color:..

Structure:..

Clarity:..

Aroma:..

Taste:..

Food pairings:..

....

....

Additional notes:..

....

....

Overall rating:

Drinkable   Recommended   Fantastic

Tualatin Estate Vineyards (Andrea Johnson Photography)

Green grapes on the vine (© Wico|Dreamstime.com)

Notes

BRITISH COLUMBIA

Main Varietals

Merlot · Pinot Noir · Cabernet
Sauvignon · Chardonnay · Pinot
Gris · Gewürztraminer

Appellations

Okanagan · Similkameen ·
Fraser Valley · Vancouver
Island · Gulf Islands

Touring Highlights

Jackson-Triggs · Sumac
Ridge · Tinhorn Creek ·
Gehringer Brothers · Wild
Goose · Kettle Valley · Blue
Mountain · CedarCreek ·
La Frenz · Quails' Gate

Vineyard field (© Csp/Dreamstime.com)

BRITISH COLUMBIA

Grapes grow in many pockets of British Columbia's farmland. The area is home to some of the best vineyards in all of Canada, and the gem of the region is the Okanagan Valley, encompassing 96 percent of British Columbia's vineyards.

The Okanagan Valley is the northerly extension of the Pacific Northwest and boasts significant climatic differences from north to south. The cooler northern climate in Okanagan's Kelowna area has perfect conditions for growing grapes that ripen early: Pinot Blanc, Pinot Gris, Pinot Noir, Riesling, and Gewürztraminer. The warmer climate to the south is suitable for grapes that ripen later, such as the red Bordeaux varieties Merlot, Cabernet Sauvignon, and Syrah. It's much like the difference between the sun-baked south of France and the cooler Burgundy region.

The Okanagan Valley AVA

The Okanagan Valley is located in southern British Columbia in a rain shadow (an area of dry land that lies on the downwind side of a mountain) between the Coastal and Monashee Mountains. The valley has about 80 miles (6,600 acres) of vineyards and is made up of five sub-appellations: Kelowna, Naramata, Okanagan Falls, Golden Mile, and Black Sage/Osoyoos.

Okanagan's variable climate presents a unique opportunity to maximize wine production in the coldest of times. Frozen grapes on the vine sound like a winemaker's worst nightmare; however, the opposite is true: the cold winters of north Okanagan's offer ideal conditions for producing the array of ice wines that make the area the unequivocal Northwest leader in ice-wine production and the world's leading exporter of this expensive dessert wine.

Though Riesling tends to be the most common grape used, ice wines can be made from either white or red varietals like Pinot Blanc and Pinot Noir. Once temperatures drop to around 15°F (9.4°C), the frozen grapes left hanging on the vine are harvested in the middle of the night. The grapes are pressed while the water crystals within the grapes are frozen solid, yielding mere drops of precious juice. While the resulting sugar levels are highly concentrated, so too are the acid levels. This is the defining characteristic of an ice wine versus a sweet wine; an ice wine is balanced and expressive, exhibiting fresh, clean, lively flavors.

Although it is best known for its ice wine, the Okanagan Valley continues to define itself as one of the most diverse wine regions in the world. With the valley's variety of soil conditions, temperatures, and elevations, large-volume wine production is difficult, but the benefits to Okanagan's niche wines are tremendous. Winemakers in the region experiment with more than 60 grape varietals from Auxerrois to Zweigelt. Stylistically, the range of wines produced is staggering: from traditional and popular favorites like Pinot Gris, Merlot, and Riesling to the delicate herbal aromas of Siegerrebe or Bacchus to the funky earthiness of Syrah and wild exoticism of Viognier. The most popular white varietals include Chardonnay and Pinot Gris, while Merlot, Pinot Noir, and blends are the reds of choice.

Inniskillin Vineyard wine barrels (Phillip Chin)

Nk'Mip Cellars (photo courtesy of Nk'Mip Cellars)

British Columbia Wineries to Visit

Name:..

Location:...

Recommended by:...

Why go:..

....

....

Name:..

Location:...

Recommended by:...

Why go:..

....

....

Name:..

Location:...

Recommended by:...

Why go:..

....

....

Name:..

Location:...

Recommended by:...

Why go:..

....

Name:..

Location:..

Recommended by:..

Why go:..

....

....

Name:..

Location:..

Recommended by:..

Why go:..

....

....

Name:..

Location:..

Recommended by:..

Why go:..

....

....

Name:..

Location:..

Recommended by:..

Why go:..

....

Name:..

Location:..

Recommended by:...

Why go:...

....

....

Name:..

Location:..

Recommended by:...

Why go:...

....

....

Name:..

Location:..

Recommended by:...

Why go:...

....

....

Name:..

Location:..

Recommended by:...

Why go:...

....

Name:..

Location:...

Recommended by:...

Why go:...

....

....

Name:..

Location:...

Recommended by:...

Why go:...

....

....

Name:..

Location:...

Recommended by:...

Why go:...

....

....

Name:..

Location:...

Recommended by:...

Why go:...

....

Name:..

Location:..

Recommended by:..

Why go:..

....

....

Name:..

Location:..

Recommended by:..

Why go:..

....

....

Name:..

Location:..

Recommended by:..

Why go:..

....

....

Name:..

Location:..

Recommended by:..

Why go:..

....

Name:...

Location:..

Recommended by:..

Why go:..

....

....

Name:...

Location:..

Recommended by:..

Why go:..

....

....

Name:...

Location:..

Recommended by:..

Why go:..

....

....

Name:...

Location:..

Recommended by:..

Why go:..

....

British Columbia Reds

Winery:...

Region:...

Name of wine:...

Vintage:..

Price:..

Purchase date:...

Circle:

Cabernet Sauvignon	Cabernet Franc	Gamay Grenache
Merlot	Nebbiolo	Pinot Noir
Syrah	Sangiovese	Tempranillo
Zinfandel	Other.........................	

Color:...

Structure:...

Aroma:..

Taste:..

Food pairings:...

....

....

Additional notes:..

....

....

Overall rating:

Drinkable   Recommended   Fantastic

British Columbia Reds

Winery:...

Region:...

Name of wine:...

Vintage:...

Price:...

Purchase date:..

Circle:

Cabernet Sauvignon	Cabernet Franc	Gamay Grenache
Merlot	Nebbiolo	Pinot Noir
Syrah	Sangiovese	Tempranillo
Zinfandel	Other.........................	

Color:..

Structure:..

Aroma:..

Taste:..

Food pairings:...

....

....

Additional notes:..

....

....

Overall rating:

Drinkable   Recommended   Fantastic

British Columbia Reds

Winery:..

Region:..

Name of wine:...

Vintage:..

Price:..

Purchase date:..

Circle:

Cabernet Sauvignon	Cabernet Franc	Gamay Grenache
Merlot	Nebbiolo	Pinot Noir
Syrah	Sangiovese	Tempranillo
Zinfandel	Other...........................	

Color:...

Structure:...

Aroma:...

Taste:...

Food pairings:...

....

....

Additional notes:..

....

....

Overall rating:

Drinkable   Recommended   Fantastic

British Columbia Reds

Winery:..

Region:..

Name of wine:...

Vintage:..

Price:..

Purchase date:...

Circle:

Cabernet Sauvignon	Cabernet Franc	Gamay Grenache
Merlot	Nebbiolo	Pinot Noir
Syrah	Sangiovese	Tempranillo
Zinfandel	Other.........................	

Color:..

Structure:..

Aroma:...

Taste:..

Food pairings:..

....

....

Additional notes:...

....

....

Overall rating:

Drinkable   Recommended   Fantastic

British Columbia Reds

Winery:...

Region:..

Name of wine:..

Vintage:..

Price:..

Purchase date:...

Circle:

Cabernet Sauvignon	Cabernet Franc	Gamay Grenache
Merlot	Nebbiolo	Pinot Noir
Syrah	Sangiovese	Tempranillo
Zinfandel	Other........................	

Color:...

Structure:..

Aroma:..

Taste:..

Food pairings:..

....

....

Additional notes:..

....

....

Overall rating:

Drinkable   Recommended   Fantastic

British Columbia Reds

Winery:...

Region:...

Name of wine:...

Vintage:...

Price:...

Purchase date:..

Circle:

Cabernet Sauvignon	Cabernet Franc	Gamay Grenache
Merlot	Nebbiolo	Pinot Noir
Syrah	Sangiovese	Tempranillo
Zinfandel	Other..........................	

Color:..

Structure:..

Aroma:...

Taste:...

Food pairings:...

....

....

Additional notes:..

....

....

Overall rating:

Drinkable	Recommended	Fantastic

British Columbia Reds

Winery:...

Region:..

Name of wine:...

Vintage:...

Price:...

Purchase date:...

Circle:

Cabernet Sauvignon	Cabernet Franc	Gamay Grenache
Merlot	Nebbiolo	Pinot Noir
Syrah	Sangiovese	Tempranillo
Zinfandel	Other........................	

Color:..

Structure:..

Aroma:..

Taste:...

Food pairings:...

....

....

Additional notes:..

....

....

Overall rating:

Drinkable   Recommended   Fantastic

British Columbia Reds

Winery:..

Region:..

Name of wine:..

Vintage:..

Price:...

Purchase date:...

Circle:

Cabernet Sauvignon	Cabernet Franc	Gamay Grenache
Merlot	Nebbiolo	Pinot Noir
Syrah	Sangiovese	Tempranillo
Zinfandel	Other........................	

Color:...

Structure:...

Aroma:...

Taste:..

Food pairings:...

....

....

Additional notes:...

....

....

Overall rating:

Drinkable   Recommended   Fantastic

British Columbia Reds

Winery:..

Region:..

Name of wine:..

Vintage:..

Price:..

Purchase date:..

Circle:

Cabernet Sauvignon	Cabernet Franc	Gamay Grenache
Merlot	Nebbiolo	Pinot Noir
Syrah	Sangiovese	Tempranillo
Zinfandel	Other........................	

Color:...

Structure:...

Aroma:...

Taste:...

Food pairings:..

....

....

Additional notes:...

....

....

Overall rating:

Drinkable   Recommended   Fantastic

British Columbia Reds

Winery:..

Region:..

Name of wine:..

Vintage:..

Price:..

Purchase date:...

Circle:

Cabernet Sauvignon	Cabernet Franc	Gamay Grenache
Merlot	Nebbiolo	Pinot Noir
Syrah	Sangiovese	Tempranillo
Zinfandel	Other..........................	

Color:...

Structure:..

Aroma:..

Taste:..

Food pairings:..

....

....

Additional notes:...

....

....

Overall rating:

Drinkable   Recommended   Fantastic

British Columbia Reds

Winery:..

Region:..

Name of wine:..

Vintage:..

Price:..

Purchase date:...

Circle:

Cabernet Sauvignon	Cabernet Franc	Gamay Grenache
Merlot	Nebbiolo	Pinot Noir
Syrah	Sangiovese	Tempranillo
Zinfandel	Other.........................	

Color:...

Structure:..

Aroma:..

Taste:...

Food pairings:...

....

....

Additional notes:...

....

....

Overall rating:

Drinkable   Recommended   Fantastic

British Columbia Reds

Winery:...

Region:...

Name of wine:...

Vintage:..

Price:..

Purchase date:..

Circle:

Cabernet Sauvignon	Cabernet Franc	Gamay Grenache
Merlot	Nebbiolo	Pinot Noir
Syrah	Sangiovese	Tempranillo
Zinfandel	Other..........................	

Color:...

Structure:..

Aroma:...

Taste:...

Food pairings:...

....

....

Additional notes:..

....

....

Overall rating:

Drinkable   Recommended   Fantastic

British Columbia Reds

Winery:..

Region:..

Name of wine:..

Vintage:..

Price:..

Purchase date:..

Circle:

Cabernet Sauvignon	Cabernet Franc	Gamay Grenache
Merlot	Nebbiolo	Pinot Noir
Syrah	Sangiovese	Tempranillo
Zinfandel	Other..........................	

Color:...

Structure:...

Aroma:..

Taste:..

Food pairings:..

....

....

Additional notes:..

....

....

Overall rating:

Drinkable   Recommended   Fantastic

British Columbia Reds

Winery:...

Region:...

Name of wine:..

Vintage:...

Price:...

Purchase date:...

Circle:

Cabernet Sauvignon	Cabernet Franc	Gamay Grenache
Merlot	Nebbiolo	Pinot Noir
Syrah	Sangiovese	Tempranillo
Zinfandel	Other...........................	

Color:..

Structure:..

Aroma:...

Taste:...

Food pairings:..

....

....

Additional notes:...

....

....

Overall rating:

Drinkable   Recommended   Fantastic

SunRock Vineyard (Brian Sprout)

Winemaker Mark Wenenburg, Suma Ridge (Phillip Chin)

British Columbia Whites

Winery:...

Region:...

Name of wine:...

Vintage:...

Price:...

Purchase date:..

Circle:

Chardonnay	Chenin Blanc	Gewürztraminer	Muscat
Pinot Gris	Riesling	Sauvignon Blanc	Sémillon
Viognier	Other.........................		

Color:...

Structure:..

Clarity:...

Aroma:...

Taste:..

Food pairings:...

....

....

Additional notes:..

....

....

Overall rating:

Drinkable   Recommended   Fantastic

British Columbia Whites

Winery:..

Region:..

Name of wine:..

Vintage:...

Price:...

Purchase date:...

Circle:

Chardonnay	Chenin Blanc	Gewürztraminer	Muscat
Pinot Gris	Riesling	Sauvignon Blanc	Sémillon
Viognier	Other........................		

Color:..

Structure:..

Clarity:..

Aroma:..

Taste:...

Food pairings:...

....

....

Additional notes:..

....

....

Overall rating:

Drinkable   Recommended   Fantastic

British Columbia Whites

Winery:...

Region:...

Name of wine:...

Vintage:...

Price:...

Purchase date:..

Circle:

Chardonnay	Chenin Blanc	Gewürztraminer	Muscat
Pinot Gris	Riesling	Sauvignon Blanc	Sémillon
Viognier	Other........................		

Color:..

Structure:..

Clarity:..

Aroma:...

Taste:...

Food pairings:...

....

....

Additional notes:..

....

....

Overall rating:

Drinkable   Recommended   Fantastic

British Columbia Whites

Winery:..

Region:..

Name of wine:..

Vintage:...

Price:...

Purchase date:...

Circle:

Chardonnay	Chenin Blanc	Gewürztraminer	Muscat
Pinot Gris	Riesling	Sauvignon Blanc	Sémillon
Viognier	Other.........................		

Color:..

Structure:...

Clarity:..

Aroma:...

Taste:...

Food pairings:..

....

....

Additional notes:..

....

....

Overall rating:

Drinkable   Recommended   Fantastic

British Columbia Whites

Winery:..

Region:..

Name of wine:..

Vintage:...

Price:...

Purchase date:..

Circle:

Chardonnay	Chenin Blanc	Gewürztraminer	Muscat
Pinot Gris	Riesling	Sauvignon Blanc	Sémillon
Viognier	Other..........................		

Color:...

Structure:...

Clarity:...

Aroma:...

Taste:...

Food pairings:...

....

....

Additional notes:...

....

....

Overall rating:

Drinkable   Recommended   Fantastic

British Columbia Whites

Winery:..

Region:...

Name of wine:..

Vintage:..

Price:..

Purchase date:...

Circle:

Chardonnay	Chenin Blanc	Gewürztraminer	Muscat
Pinot Gris	Riesling	Sauvignon Blanc	Sémillon
Viognier	Other........................		

Color:...

Structure:...

Clarity:...

Aroma:..

Taste:..

Food pairings:..

....

....

Additional notes:...

....

....

Overall rating:

Drinkable   Recommended   Fantastic

British Columbia Whites

Winery:...

Region:...

Name of wine:...

Vintage:...

Price:...

Purchase date:...

Circle:

Chardonnay	Chenin Blanc	Gewürztraminer	Muscat
Pinot Gris	Riesling	Sauvignon Blanc	Sémillon
Viognier	Other.........................		

Color:...

Structure:...

Clarity:..

Aroma:...

Taste:...

Food pairings:...

....

....

Additional notes:..

....

....

Overall rating:

Drinkable   Recommended   Fantastic

British Columbia Whites

Winery:...

Region:...

Name of wine:..

Vintage:...

Price:...

Purchase date:..

Circle:

Chardonnay	Chenin Blanc	Gewürztraminer	Muscat
Pinot Gris	Riesling	Sauvignon Blanc	Sémillon
Viognier	Other......................		

Color:..

Structure:..

Clarity:..

Aroma:..

Taste:..

Food pairings:..

....

....

Additional notes:...

....

....

Overall rating:

Drinkable   Recommended   Fantastic

British Columbia Whites

Winery:...

Region:...

Name of wine:...

Vintage:...

Price:..

Purchase date:...

Circle:

Chardonnay	Chenin Blanc	Gewürztraminer	Muscat
Pinot Gris	Riesling	Sauvignon Blanc	Sémillon
Viognier	Other........................		

Color:..

Structure:...

Clarity:..

Aroma:..

Taste:...

Food pairings:..

....

....

Additional notes:..

....

....

Overall rating:

Drinkable   Recommended   Fantastic

British Columbia Whites

Winery:..

Region:..

Name of wine:..

Vintage:...

Price:..

Purchase date:...

Circle:

Chardonnay	Chenin Blanc	Gewürztraminer	Muscat
Pinot Gris	Riesling	Sauvignon Blanc	Sémillon
Viognier	Other..........................		

Color:..

Structure:..

Clarity:..

Aroma:..

Taste:..

Food pairings:..

....

....

Additional notes:...

....

....

Overall rating:

Drinkable   Recommended   Fantastic

British Columbia Whites

Winery:..

Region:..

Name of wine:..

Vintage:..

Price:..

Purchase date:..

Circle:

Chardonnay	Chenin Blanc	Gewürztraminer	Muscat
Pinot Gris	Riesling	Sauvignon Blanc	Sémillon
Viognier	Other........................		

Color:..

Structure:..

Clarity:..

Aroma:..

Taste:..

Food pairings:..

....

....

Additional notes:..

....

....

Overall rating:

Drinkable   Recommended   Fantastic

British Columbia Whites

Winery:...

Region:...

Name of wine:...

Vintage:...

Price:...

Purchase date:...

Circle:

Chardonnay   Chenin Blanc   Gewürztraminer   Muscat

Pinot Gris   Riesling   Sauvignon Blanc   Sémillon

Viognier   Other.........................

Color:..

Structure:...

Clarity:..

Aroma:..

Taste:..

Food pairings:...

....

....

Additional notes:...

....

....

Overall rating:

Drinkable   Recommended   Fantastic

British Columbia Whites

Winery:..

Region:..

Name of wine:...

Vintage:..

Price:...

Purchase date:...

Circle:

Chardonnay	Chenin Blanc	Gewürztraminer	Muscat
Pinot Gris	Riesling	Sauvignon Blanc	Sémillon
Viognier	Other........................		

Color:...

Structure:..

Clarity:..

Aroma:..

Taste:...

Food pairings:..

....

....

Additional notes:...

....

....

Overall rating:

Drinkable   Recommended   Fantastic

British Columbia Whites

Winery:..

Region:..

Name of wine:...

Vintage:..

Price:..

Purchase date:...

Circle:

Chardonnay   Chenin Blanc   Gewürztraminer   Muscat
Pinot Gris   Riesling   Sauvignon Blanc   Sémillon
Viognier   Other.........................

Color:...

Structure:...

Clarity:...

Aroma:...

Taste:...

Food pairings:...

....

....

Additional notes:..

....

....

Overall rating:

Drinkable   Recommended   Fantastic

Notes

WASHINGTON WINERIES

For more information about Washington wineries, visit www.washingtonwine.org

428
Abeja
Adamant Cellars
Adams Bench
Adytum Cellars
Agate Field Vineyard
Airfield Estates Winery/Airport Ranch
   Winery
Airport Ranches, Inc.
Alexandria Nicole Cellars
ALIA Wines
Almquist Family Cellars
aMaurice Cellars
Amavi Cellars
Andrake Cellars
Animale
Anna Marie Vineyard
Anton Ville Winery
Apex Cellars
Arbor Crest Wine Cellars
Arlington Road Cellars
Ash Hollow
Austin Robaire Vintners
Avery Lane
Bad Seed Cider House
Badger Mountain Vineyard
Baer Winery
Bainbridge Islands Vineyards & Winery
Balboa Winery
Balcom & Moe, Inc.
Balsamroot Winery & Vineyard
Barnard Griffin Winery
Barrage Cellars
Barrelstone
Barrister Winery
Basalt Cellars
Basel Cellars Estate Winery
Benke Cellars

Benson Vineyards Estate Winery
Bergevin Lane Vineyards
Berghof Keller
Betz Family Winery
Big Pine Winery
Biscuit Ridge Vineyards
Black Diamond Winery
Black River Winery
Blackwood Canyon Vintners
Blooms
Bodega Turner Winery
Bonair Winery
Bookwalter Winery
Boudreaux Cellars
Bowman Orchards
Bradenview Vineyards
Brian Carter Cellars
Bridgman Cellars
Buckmaster Cellars
Bunchgrass Winery
Bunnell Family Cellar
Buty
C.I. Cellars/Columbia Industries
C.R. Sandidge Wines
Cadence
Camano Cellars
Camaraderie Cellars
Cannon Hill Vintners
Canoe Ridge Vineyard
Canyon River Ranch
Canyon's Edge Winery
Capstone Cellars
Carpenter Creek Winery
Cascade Cliffs Vineyard & Winery
Cascadia Winery
Castle Bridge Winery
Cavatappi Winery
Cave B Estate Winery

Cawley Vineyard
Cayuse Vineyards
Celebration Wines
Challenger Ridge Vineyards & Cellars
Champoux Vineyards, LLC
Chandler Reach Vineyards
Chateau Champoux Tours & Tasting
Chateau Faire Le Pont
Chateau Rollat Winery
Chateau Ste. Michelle
Chatter Creek Winery
Chelan Estate Winery & Vineyards
Chelan Ridge
Chelangr'La
Chester-Kidder
Chinook Wines
Christina James Winery
Christopher Cellars
Chuckanut Ridge Wine Company
Claar Cellars
Classic Winemakers
Coates Winery
Col Solare
College Cellars of Walla Walla
Columbia Crest
Columbia Valley Wine Warehouse
Columbia Winery
Colvin Vineyards
Copper Mountain Vineyards
Corus Estates & Vineyards
Cougar Creek Wine
Cougar Crest Winery
Cougar Hills Vineyard
Covey Run Winery
Covington Cellars
Cowan Vineyards
Coyote Canyon Winery
Cuillin Hills Winery
Dakota Creek Winery
Daven Lore Winery
DeLille Cellars and Doyenne
Des Voigne Cellars
Desert Hills
Desert Wind Winery

DiStefano Winery
Domaine Pierre Noire
Domaine Ste. Michelle
Domanico Cellars
Donitelia Winery
DuBrul Vineyards
Dunham Cellars
Dusted Valley Vintners
E.B. Foote Winery
Eagle Haven Winery
Eaglemount Wine and Cider
Eaton Hill Winery
Echo Cellars
Eclaire Vineyards
Edmonds Winery
Efeste
El Mirador Winery
Elephant Mountain Vineyards
Eleven
Empryean Wines
English Estate Winery
Ensemble Cellars
Eroica
Evergreen Vineyards
The Estates
Facelli Winery
Fall Line Winery
Feather
Fidélitas
Fielding Hills Winery
Figgins Estate
Firesteed Cellars
Five Star Cellars
Foolish Oak
Forgeron Cellars
Fort Walla Walla Cellars
Foundry Vineyards
Four Lakes Chelan
Frenchman Hills Winery
Frye Winery
Galitzine Vineyard
Gallaghers Where U-Brew
Gamache Vintners
Garrison Creek Cellars

Gibbons Lane Winery
Gifford Hirlinger
Gilbert Cellars
Ginkgo Forest Winery
Glacial Lake Missoula Wine Company
Glacier Peak Vineyard
Glen Fiona Winery
Goose Ridge Estate Vineyards and
  Winery
Gordon Brothers
Gorge Crest Winery
Gramercy Cellars
Grande Ronde Cellars
Graves Cellars
Graves Vineyard
Greenbank Cellars
Griffins Crossing Winery
Guardian Cellars
Harbinger Winery
Harlequin Wine Cellars
Heaven's Cave Cellars
Hedges Bel' Villa Estates
Hedges Family Estate
Hence Cellars
Heymann Whinery
Hi Oasis Orchards
Hightower Cellars
Hinzerling Winery
Hogue Cellars
Hogue Ranches
Hollywood Hill Vineyards and
  Eastside Winery
Holtzinger Fruit Co.
Hoodsport Winery
Hoover & Roofus
Hope Vineyards
Horizon's Edge Winery
Huck
Hurricane Ridge Winery
Hyatt Vineyards
Icicle Ridge Winery
Illusion Winery
Isabella Grace Winery
Isenhower Cellars

Januik Winery
JLC Winery
JM Cellars
Jones Of Washington
JPJ Family Enterprises
Ju'lianne Cellars
Kana Winery
Kestrel Leavenworth Tasting Room
Kestrel Vintners
Kiona Vineyards Winery
Kludt Family Winery
Konnowac Vineyards
Kyra Wines
L'Ecole N° 41
Lahar Winery
Laht Neppur Cellars
Lake Crest Winery
Lantz Cellars
Latah Creek Wine Cellars
Latitude 46° North
Legoe Bay Winery
Leonetti Cellar
Les Collines Vineyard
Lodmell Cellars
Lone Canary
Long Shadows Vintners
Lopez Island Vineyards
Lost Mountain Winery
Lost River Winery
Lowden Hills Winery
Mad Car Wine Company
Madsen Family Cellars
The Magnificent Wine Company
Maison de Padgett Winery
Major Creek Cellars
Mannina Cellars
Market Cellar Winery
Marshal's Winery
Martin-Scott Winery
Maryhill Winery
Masquerade Wine Company
Masset Winery
Matthews Cellars
McCormick Family Vineyards

McCrea Cellars
McGavick Nanstad Winery
McKinley Springs Winery
Meek Family Estate
Mercer Estates Winery
Merry Cellars
Michaela's Vineyard
Michelle Loosen
Milbrandt Vineyards Winery
Misty Isle Vineyard
Morchella Wine Cellars
Mount Baker Vineyards
Mrachek Vineyards
Naches Heights Vineyard & Winery
Naked Winery
Napeequa Vintners
Nefarious Cellars
Neff Cellars
Nelms Road
Nicholas Cole Cellars
Nodland Cellars
North Shore Wine Cellars
Northstar Winery
Northwest Cellars
Northwest Totem Cellars
Norton Arnold Vintners
Nota Bene Cellars
Novelty Hill Winery
O. S. Winery
Oakwood Cellars
Okanogan Estate & Vineyards
Olsen Estates
Olympic Cellars
Otis Kenyon Wine
Pacific Rim
Page Cellars
Painted Ladder Estates
Pangaea Winery
Paradisos del Sol
Pasek Cellars Winery
Patit Creek Cellars
Patrick M. Paul Vineyards
Paul Thomas Winery
Pavin & Riley

Pedestal
Pendulum
Pepper Bridge Winery
Perennial Vintners
Phinny Hill Vintners
Piety Flats Winery
Pine & Post
Pirouette
Poet's Leap
Poiesis Wines
Pomum Cellars
Portrait Cellars
Portteus
Powers Winery
Preston Premium Wines
Prosser Wine Company
Quilceda Creek Vintners
Rainey Valley Winery
Rainier Ridge
Randall Harris
Red Diamond
Red Sky Winery
Reininger Winery
Renaissance Cellar
Revelry Vintners
RiverAerie
RMV Cellars
Robert Karl Cellars
Rockmeadow Cellars
RockWall Cellars
Ross Andrew Winery
Roza Hills Vineyard
Running Springs Wine
Russell Creek Winery
Rustygrape Vineyards
Ryan Patrick Vineyards
Sagelands Vineyard
Sagemoor Vineyards
Saggi
Saint Laurent Winery
Saintpaulia Vintners
Samson Estates Winery
Sandhill Winery
Sapolil Cellars Winery

Sapphire Mountain Cellars
Saviah Cellars
Scott Family Winery
Seia Wine Cellars
Sequel
Seven Hills Winery
Severino Cellars
Shady Grove Winery
Sheridan Vineyard
Shimmer
Silver Lake Winery
Silver Lake Winery at Roza Hills
Sky River Meadery
Skylite Cellars
Sleeping Dog Wines
Sleeping Giant Winery
Sleight of Hand Cellars
Snoqualmie Vineyards
Sockeye
Sol Duc
Soos Creek Wine Cellars
Sorensen Cellars
Sovereign Cellars
Sparkman Cellars
Spring Valley Vineyard
Spyder Lake Winery and Wine Shop
St. Hilaire Cellars
Stemilt Creek Winery
Stephenson Cellars
Steppe Cellars
Stevens Winery
Stina's Cellars
Stonecap—Monson Family Estates
Sunset Vineyards
Sweet Pea
Syncline
SYZYGY
Tagaris Winery
Tamarack Cellars
Tanjuli
Tapteil Vineyard
Tefft Cellars
Terra Blanca Winery & Estate Vineyard
Tertulia Cellars

Three Brothers Vineyard & Winery
Three Rivers Winery
Thurston Wolfe Winery
Tiger Mountain Winery
Tildio Winery
TMW Vineyards
Trillium Creek Winery
Trio Vintners
Trust Cellars
Tsillan Cellars
Tucker Cellars Winery
Tunnel Hill Winery
Two Dragons
Two Mountain Winery
Tytonidae Cellars
Upland Vineyards & Winery
Va Piano Vineyards
Vashon Winery
Ventimiglia Cellars
Vin du Lac Winery
Vine & Sun
Vinesmith's Cellar
Vintage Hill Cellars
Wahluke Wine Company
Waliser Winery & Vineyard
Walla Walla Cellars
Walla Walla Village Winery
Walla Walla Vintners
Walter Dacon Wines
Ward Johnson Winery
Washington Hills
Washington Vintners
Waterbrook Winery
Waters Winery
Waterville Wine Company
Wautoma Springs Vineyard
Waving Tree Vineyards & Winery
Wawawai Canyon
Weatherwax Cellars
Wedge Mountain Winery
Westcott Bay Orchards
Westport Winery
Whatcom Winemakers
Whidbey Island Vineyard & Winery

White Heron Cellars
White Salmon Vineyard
Whitestone Winery & Vineyard
Whitman Cellars
Widgeon Hill Winery
William Church Winery
Willis Hall
Willow Crest Winery
Wilridge Winery
Wind River Cellars
Windfall Winery
Windy Point Vineyards

Wineglass Cellars
The Winemaker's Loft
Wines of Substance
Woodhouse Family Cellars
Woodinville Wine Cellars
Woodward Canyon Winery
Wrangler
XS Vintners
Yakima Cellars
Yakima River Winery
Yellow Hawk Cellar

OREGON WINERIES

For more information about Oregon wineries, visit oregonwine.org

12 Ranch Wines
Abacela Vineyards & Winery
Abiqua Wind Vineyard
Academy Wines
ADEA Wine Company
Adelsheim Vineyard
Agate Ridge Vineyard
Airlie Winery
Alloro Vineyard
Amalie Robert Estate
Amity Vineyards
Anam Cara Cellars
Anderson Family Vineyard
Andrew Rich Wines
Anindor Vineyards
Ankeny Vineyard Winery
Anne Amie Vineyards
Anthony Dell Cellars
Antica Terra
Apolloni Vineyards
Appellation Oregon
Applegate Red Winery
Aramenta Cellars
ArborBrook Vineyards
Arcane Cellars
Archery Summit
Argyle Winery
Atticus Wine
August Cellars
Ayoub Vineyard
Ayres Vineyard and Winery
Barbara Thomas Wines
Barking Frog Winery
Bear Creek Winery
Beaux Frères
Bella Vida Vineyard
Belle Pente Vineyards and Winery
Belle Vallée Cellars

Benton-Lane Winery
Beran Vineyards
Bergström
Bethel Heights Vineyard
Bishop Creek Cellars
Black Cap of Oregon
Boedecker Cellars
Bradley Vineyards
Brandborg Vineyard & Winery
Brick House Wine Company
Bridgeview Winery
Broadley Vineyards
Brooks Wines
Bryce Vineyard
Bryn Mawr Vineyards
Cana's Feast
Cana's Feast Winery
Carabella Vineyard
Cardwell Hill Cellars
Carlo & Julian
Carlton Cellars
Carlton Winemakers Studio
Carpenter Hill Vineyards
Cathedral Ridge Winery
Champoeg Wine Cellars
Chateau Bianca Winery
Chateau Lorane
Chehalem
Cherry Hill Winery
Christopher Bridge Cellars and Satori
    Springs Vineyard
Cliff Creek Wines/Sams Valley Vineyard
Cloudrest Vineyards
Coelho Winery of Amity
Coeur de Terre Vineyard
Coleman Vineyard
Cooper Mountain Vineyards
The Cost Vineyard

Crater Lake Cellars
Cricket Hill Winery
Cristom Vineyards
Cubanisimo Vineyards
Daedalus Cellars
Daisy Creek Vineyard
Dalla Vina Wines
David Hill Vineyard and Winery
de Lancellotti Vineyards
De Ponte Cellars
Del Rio Vineyards
Delfino Vineyards
Devitt Winery & Vineyards
Dobbes Family Estate
Domaine Coteau
Domaine Drouhin Oregon
Domaine Meriwether
Domaine Serene Winery
Duck Pond Cellars
Durant Vineyards
Dusky Goose
EdenVale Winery
Edgefield Winery
EIEIO & Company
Elk Cove Vineyards
Elkhorn Ridge Vineyards and Winery
ElvenGlade Vineyard
Emerson Vineyards
Eola Hills Wine Cellars
Erath Vineyards
Erin Glenn Vineyards
Et Fille Wines
Eugene Wine Cellars
Evergreen Vineyards
Evesham Wood Vineyard
The Eyrie Vineyards
Ferraro Cellar
Folin Cellars
Foris Vineyards Winery
The Four Graces
Francis Tannahill
Freja Cellars
Fruithill Inc.
Girardet Wine Cellars

Greenwood Vineyard
Gypsy Dancer Estates
Hamacher Wines
Harris Bridge Vineyard
Hauer of the Dauen
Helvetia Vineyards and Winery
Henry Estate Winery
Hillcrest Vineyard
Hip Chicks do Wine
Honeywood Winery
Hood River Vineyards
Iris Hill Winery
J. Albin Winery
J.K. Carriere Wines
John Michael Champagne Cellars and
    Nicholas Vineyards
Ken Wright Cellars
King Estate Winery
Kramer Vineyards
Kristin Hill Winery
La Bête Wines
Lachini Vineyards
Lange Estate Winery & Vineyards
Laura Volkman Vineyards
Laurel Hood
Laurel Ridge
LaVelle Vineyards
Lawton Winery
Le Cadeau Vineyard
Left Coast Cellars
Lemelson Vineyards
Lenné
Longsword Vineyard
Madrone Mountain
Marquam Hill Vineyards
Marshanne Landing
Maysara Winery
Medici Vineyards
Melrose Vineyards
Methven Family Wines
Misty Oaks Vineyards
Monks Gate Vineyard
Montinore Estate
Mt. Hood Winery

Mystic Wines
Naked Winery
Namasté Vineyards
Natalie's Estate Winery
NW Wine Company
Oak Knoll Winery
Otis Kenyon Wine
Owen Roe
Palotai Vineyard and Winery
Panther Creek Cellars
Paradis Family Vineyard
Paschal Winery & Vineyard
Patricia Green Cellars
Patton Valley Vineyard
Pebblestone Cellars
Penner-Ash Wine Cellars
Pfeiffer Vineyards
Pheasant Court Winery
Phelps Creek Vineyards
Ponzi Vineyards
Purple Cow Vineyards
R. Stuart & Co.
Raptor Ridge Winery
Redhawk Winery
Redman Vineyard & Winery
Remy Wines
Resonance Vineyard
Retour
Reustle-Prayer Rock Vineyards
Rex Hill Vineyards
Ribbon Ridge Vineyard
River's Edge Winery
Rockblock
Rosella's Vineyard and Winery
RoxyAnn Winery
RR Winery
Ruby Carbiener
Saginaw Vineyard
SakéOne
Sass Winery/Wild Winds Winery
Schmidt Family Vineyards
Scott Paul Wines
Secret House Winery
Séjourné

Seufert Winery
Shafer Vineyard Cellars
Shallon Winery
Shea Wine Cellars
Sienna Ridge Estate
Silvan Ridge-Hinman Vineyards
Sineann
Slagle Creek Vineyards
Slagle Creek Vineyards Inc.
Sokol Blosser Winery
Soléna Cellars
Soter Vineyards
Spangler Vineyards
Spindrift Cellars
Springhill Cellars
St. Innocent Winery
Stag Hollow Wines
Stangeland Winery
Stoller Vineyards
Stone Wolf Vineyards
Stony Mountain Vineyard
Styring Vineyards
Sweet Cheeks Winery
Thistle Wines
Torii Mor Vineyard and Winery
Trium
Troon Vineyard
Troon Vineyard
Twelve Wine
Tyee Wine Cellars
Tyrus Evan
Utopia Vineyard and Cellars
Valley View Winery
Van Duzer Vineyards
Vidon Vineyard, LLC
Viento
Vista Hills Vineyard
Vitae Springs Vineyard
VX (Vercingetorix) Vineyard
Walnut City Wineworks
Weisinger's of Ashland Winery
Westrey Wine Company
Wheatridge in the Nook
Whistling Dog Cellars

White Rose Wines
Wild Rose Vineyard
WildAire Cellars
Willakenzie Estate Inc.
Willamette Valley Vineyards
William Hatcher Wines
Winderlea Wine Company
Windridge Vineyards
Wine Country Farm Cellars

Winter's Hill Vineyard
Witness Tree Vineyard
Wooldridge Creek Vineyard and
  Winery
Yamhill Valley Vineyards
Youngberg Hill Vineyards
Zenas Wines
Zerba Cellars
ZIVO

BRITISH COLUMBIA WINERIES

For more information about British Columbia wineries, visit the following Web sites:

www.okanaganwines.ca

www.winebc.com

www.bcwine.ca

Alderlea Vineyards
Antelope Ridge
Arrowleaf Cellars
Bella Vista Vineyards
Black Hills Estate Winery
Blossom Winery
Blue Grouse Vineyard & Winery
Bounty Cellars
Burrowing Owl Estate Winery
Calona Vineyards
CedarCreek Estate Winery
Chateau Wolff
Church & State Winery
Columbia Gardens Winery
Crowsnest Vineyards
Desert Hills Estate Winery
Dunham & Froese Estate Winery
Gehringer Brothers Estate Winery
Granite Creek Estate Wines
Gray Monk Estate Winery
Greata Ranch Vineyards
Hainle Vineyards & Deep Creek
    Wine Estate
Herder Winery and Vineyards
Hester Creek Estate Winery
Hijas Bonitas Vineyard
Inniskillin Okanagan Vineyards
Isabella Winery Ltd.
Jackson-Triggs Vincor International
Lake Breeze Vineyards
Lang Vineyards
Le Vieux Pin Winery
Little Straw Vineyards Estate Winery
Mission Hill Family Estate Winery

Mistral Vineyards
Mt. Boucherie Estate Winery
Nk'Mip Cellars
Noble Ridge Winery
Oliver Twist Estate Winery
Osoyoos Larose Estate Winery
Paradise Ranch Wines
Peller Estates
Pinot Reach Cellars
Quails' Gate Estate Winery
Quinta Ferreira Estate Winery
Red Rooster Winery
Rollingdale Winery
Salt Spring Vineyards
Sandhill Wines
Saturna Island Family Estate Winery
See Ya Later Ranch
Soaring Eagle Estate Winery
St. Hubertus Estate Winery
St. Urban Winery
Stonehill Estate Winery
Sumac Ridge Estate Winery
Summerhill Pyramid Winery
Tantalus Vineyards
Therapy Vineyards
Thornhaven Estates Winery
Tinhorn Creek Vineyards
Township 7 Vineyards & Winery
    (Langley)
Township 7 Vineyards & Winery
    (Okanagan)
Van Westen Vineyards
Wild Goose Vineyards

About the Author

Teri Citterman is the 2008 recipient of the Editor's Choice award from the Napa Valley Wine Writers Symposium. She is a regular contributor to *Seattle Metropolitan* magazine, writes a wine column for *Wine Press Northwest* and, as an extension of the column, blogs about life paired with wine in An Urban Sip: anurbansip.blogspot.com/. Her articles have appeared in a variety of other outlets including *Puget Sound Business Journal, Portland Business Journal, Seattle Magazine,* and the *Best Places Northwest* travel guidebooks. Though home is Seattle, Teri and her husband are avid travelers and enjoy sipping their way through the world.